The Fearless Girl and The Little Guy with Greatness

Young Leaders Guide

"The Fearless Girl and the Little Guy with Greatness - Young Leaders Guide" introduces kids from ages 6 to 12 to five super skills in a fun and engaging way.

The Fearless Girl, the Little Guy with Greatness and their friends will take you on a journey to learn more about these super skills and even practice them through a very special "Try It Activity" in each section.

On the pages ahead, you will learn how to be the most creative that you can, communicate effectively, and collaborate with others. You will also learn how to adapt to change and become a great leader!

By the end of the book, you will be equipped with the skills and knowledge you need to become an even more successful and well-rounded individual.

So, are you ready to join the Fearless Girl and the Little Guy with Greatness on this exciting adventure? **Let's get started!**

Written by

**Mort Greenberg &
Carly Greenberg**

3

Copyright © 2023 by
Mort Greenberg & Carly Greenberg

Design: Heri Susanto
Illustrations: Dian Kartika Abidin

First Paperback edition May 2023

ISBN 979-8-9873618-9-4

Published by TuckEmIn
www.tuckemin.com

Introduction

Tuck Em' In Publishing is a father and daughter effort that creates and publishes books for kids. Our mission is to Motivate and Inspire. Our vision is to help kids make the most of their todays and tomorrows.

The Fearless Girl and The Little Guy with Greatness is a book series that aims to share the following message: **anything is possible for any kid if they put their mind to it.**

Kids, in our books you can find ways to handle yourselves in important, real-life situations. Caregivers, you will find ways to push your kids to be their best. Through our books, we hope to encourage families to communicate more effectively with each other.

This book, titled "**Young Leaders Guide,**" is the second book in our series. The five skills that map to each section of this book are: Creativity, Communication, Collaboration, Adaptability, and Leadership.

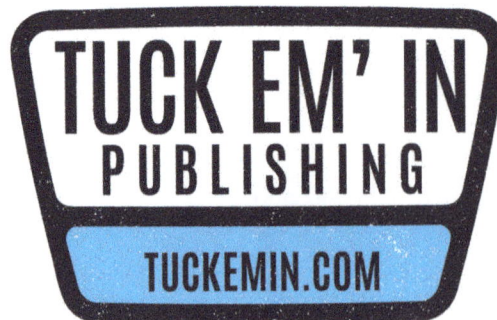

TUCK EM' IN PUBLISHING

TUCKEMIN.COM

Mort Greenberg and his daughter, **Carly Greenberg**, have embarked on numerous adventures together across the mountains of the United States. They also built self-guided, 18-hour day races in London, Paris, Milan, Venice, Murano, Burano, Rome, Buenos Aires, Tigre, Montevideo, Valparaiso, Santiago, Asuncion, and more.

This father and daughter team has worked through and overcome the same situations that you, as a parent, are experiencing now with a young daughter or son. Each skill in the book was inspired by an actual conversation that took place over the years from when Carly was five to ten years old.

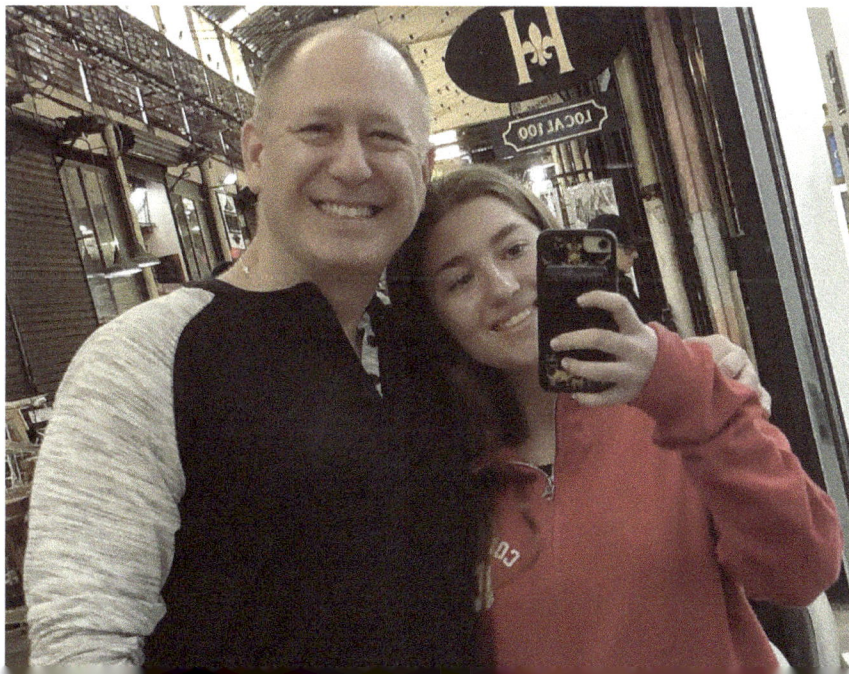

You Can Follow **Mort** and **Carly** on social media:

@mortgreenberg

@greenbergcarly

@mortgreenberg

@carlygreenberg

This Book Belongs to

_____

Today's Date : _____

Sections (Table Of Contents)

Section 01
Creativity

Imagination	11
Brainstorming	13
Inspiration	15
Experimentation	17

Section 02
Communication

Listening	23
Speaking Clearly	25
Body Language	27
Kindness	29

Section 03
Collaboration

Sharing Ideas	35
Compromise	37
Support	39

Section 04
Adaptability

Being Open-Minded	45
Problem-Solving	47
Resilience	49

Section 05
Leadership

Being a Good Role Model	55
Making Responsible Decisions	57
Communicating Effectively	59

Creativity

- Imagination
- Brainstorming
- Inspiration
- Experimentation

Creativity is the ability to come up with new and unique ideas. It's like having a superpower that helps you to think outside the box and offer up original or dynamic solutions to problems. Everyone has creativity inside them, and with enough practice, this skill can be developed and refined.

Imagination

Imagination is the first step to being creative. When you use your imagination, you can invent all sorts of ideas and possibilities. Just like a muscle, your imagination becomes stronger the more you use and exercise it.

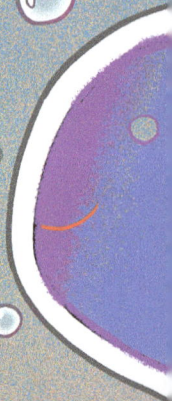

Try It Activity

Close your eyes and imagine that you are on a magical adventure. What do you see? What do you hear? What do you feel? Write down your ideas in great detail!

Brainstorming

Brainstorming is a way to come up with lots of ideas quickly. The goal is to produce as many ideas as possible, even if they may seem silly or unrealistic. Sometimes, the craziest ideas can lead to the best ones!

13

Try It Activity

Think of a problem you want to solve, like how to turn a boring day more fun. Set a timer for 5 minutes and write down as many ideas as you can. Don't worry about whether they're good or bad!

14

Inspiration

Inspiration can spring from anywhere: books, toys, movies, nature, even your own experiences. When you're inspired, you feel excited and motivated to create something new.

Try It Activity

Look around your room or outside. What inspires you or makes you excited? It could be a color, a shape, a texture, or anything else. Write down your ideas.

Experimentation

Creativity often involves trying out new things and taking risks. You might make mistakes along the way, but that's okay! It is all part of the learning process.

Try It Activity

Choose one of your ideas from the brainstorming exercise. Try it out! If it doesn't work, don't give up! Try a different idea.

"

There are absolutely no wrong answers in creativity!"

19

Creativity is a valuable skill that can help you in many areas of your life, from art and music to problem-solving and innovation. By using your imagination, brainstorming, finding inspiration, and experimenting, you can become a more creative person. Remember: there are absolutely no wrong answers in creativity!

Section 02
Communication

Listening

Speaking Clearly

Body Language

Kindness

Communication is how we share information with others. It's a way of talking to each other so that we can understand and be understood. Being a good communicator means being able to express yourself clearly and listen to others.

Listening

One of the most important parts of communication is listening. When you are listening to someone, you are paying attention to what they are saying and trying to understand their point of view. As a result, you will be able to respond back in a thoughtful and meaningful way.

Try It Activity

Find a partner and take turns telling each other a story. Then, ask the other person about their story, to make sure you understand. Then switch so that they ask you about your story.

Speaking Clearly

Speaking clearly means using words that are easy to understand as well as projecting your voice so that others can hear you.

Try It Activity

Practice speaking clearly by standing on opposite sides of the room, looking away from each other. Make sure you speak each word clearly and at a good volume so that you can understand what they are saying without being near them, or looking at them.

27

Body Language

Body language is how we use our bodies to communicate, like making eye contact or using hand motions. It can help us convey emotions and intentions. A frown means someone is angry or sad. A smile means someone is happy or excited.

Try It Activity

Play a guessing game with a partner. Act out different emotions or movements with your body. See if your partner can guess what you're trying to communicate.

Kindness

Kindness is not only being nice, but also being able to understand the feelings of others. Being kind in our thoughts, words, and questions will help you communicate more effectively because it shows that you can relate to how others are feeling.

Try It Activity

Think back on a time when you felt sad or upset. How did it make you feel when someone listened to you and showed they understood how you felt? Practice doing the same for others.

Communication is a two-way street, so it's important to both express yourself and listen to others."

Communication is an important skill that helps us connect with others and build relationships. By listening, speaking clearly, using body language, and showing kindness, you can become a better communicator. Remember: communication is a two-way street, so it's important to both express yourself and listen to others.

Collaboration

Sharing Ideas

Compromise

Support

Collaboration is working with others to achieve
a common goal. It's like teamwork, where everyone
works together to make something happen.
Being a good collaborator means being able
to work well with others.

Sharing Ideas

Collaboration involves sharing ideas
and building on each other's individual
strengths. Everyone has something
to contribute!

35

Try It Activity

Write down a problem you want to solve, like how to make a party more fun. Then, brainstorm ideas with a partner and write down all the ideas you come up with.

Compromise

In collaboration, it's important to be willing to compromise. This means finding a solution that everyone can agree on, even if it's not exactly what you would've wanted.

Try It Activity

Setting rules for a game: Create a game and work together to compromise on rules that are fair and fun for everyone. Then discuss and agree on things like how to keep score, how to handle disagreements, and how to make the game more challenging or interesting.

38

Support

Collaboration also involves supporting each other. This means helping and cheering each other on when needed.

Try It Activity

Find a partner and try to build the tallest tower you can out of blocks. Cheer each other on. Converse and help each other out whenever the tower seems to be in danger of falling. No foundation will last without support!

"

Everyone has something to contribute, and working together can lead to great things!"

Collaboration is an important skill that helps us work well with others and achieve common goals. By sharing ideas, compromising, and supporting each other, you can become a better collaborator. Remember: everyone has something to contribute, and working together can lead to great things!

Adaptability

Being Open-Minded

Problem-Solving

Resilience

Adaptability is the ability to adjust to new situations and changes. It is an important skill for navigating life's ups and downs and being able to thrive in different circumstances.

Being Open-Minded

Being open-minded is the first step in developing adaptability. In other words, be willing to consider new ideas and perspectives, even if they are different from your own.

Try It Activity

Encourage yourself to try new things, such as a new food or activity you haven't tried before. Tell your friends or parents how it feels to try something new and how you are expanding your horizons.

Problem-Solving

Problem-solving is another important aspect of adaptability. It means being able to find creative solutions to challenges that arise.

Try It Activity

Practice problem-solving by coming up with different ways to solve a puzzle or game. Encourage yourself to think outside the box and try new approaches.

Resilience

Resilience is the ability to bounce back from setbacks and challenges. It is a crucial part of adaptability, as it allows us to learn from our experiences and grow even stronger.

Try It Activity

Think about a time when you faced a challenge or setback. Ask yourself how you were able to overcome it and what you learned from the experience.

"

Adaptability is a valuable skill that can help you grow and thrive, no matter what challenges you may face."

Developing adaptability takes practice and patience, but it's an important skill that can help you navigate life's challenges and changes. By being open-minded, problem-solving, and building resilience, you can become more adaptable and better equipped to handle whatever life throws your way. Remember: adaptability is a valuable skill that can help you grow and thrive, no matter what challenges you may face.

Leadership

- Being A Good Role Model
- Making Responsible Decisions
- Communicating Effectively

Leadership is the ability to guide and inspire others towards a common goal. It involves being a good role model, making responsible decisions, and communicating effectively.

Being a Good Role Model

Being a good role model is an important part of leadership. It means setting a good example for others to follow, whether it's being honest, respectful, or hardworking.

Try It Activity

Think about someone you really admire, such as a teacher or family member. Identify the qualities that you admire in that person and how you can apply those qualities to your own life.

Making Responsible Decisions

Making responsible decisions is another important aspect of leadership. It means considering the impact of our actions on ourselves and others.

Try It Activity

Think about a decision you need to make, such as choosing between two activities or deciding what to eat for dinner. Consider the consequences of each choice and make the decision that's best for you and those around you.

Communicating Effectively

Communicating effectively is key to being a good leader. It means being able to listen to others, express our own thoughts and ideas clearly, and work collaboratively.

"

Leadership is about inspiring and guiding others towards a common goal, and you have the potential to be a great leader!"

Being a good leader takes practice and effort, but it's a valuable skill that can help you succeed in many aspects of your life.
By being a good role model, making responsible decisions, and communicating effectively, you can become a better leader and make a positive impact on those around you. Remember, leadership is about inspiring and guiding others towards a common goal, and you have the potential to be a great leader!

Conclusion

The journey of The Fearless Girl and the Little Guy with Greatness and their friends has taught you about the importance of developing super skills that will help you succeed in today's world.

These five super skills are essential for kids and will help you achieve academic success, prepare you for future careers, and foster personal growth.

By focusing on these skills, you can become better communicators, collaborators, and leaders. You also learned a little more about how to be more adaptable and what it takes to be a great leader.

With some practice, you can further develop your super skills!

Asking Awesome Questions

About The Authors

For the past 25 years **Mort Greenberg** has been a salesperson and sales manager for technology start-ups and larger media companies. Fighting his way up from an Account Executive to a role as a division President you can guess there were many challenges that needed to be overcome. Along the way Mort launched two companies, FitAd and MindFlight and learned many hard-fought lessons that start-ups are not always successful. He is a graduate of the State University of New York at New Paltz where he studied International Relations and Economics. While in college he started a company selling screen printing and promotional items to local businesses and on-campus organizations. At the same time, he also volunteered as a Congressional District Intern for the U.S. House of Representatives. He is an Eagle Scout and in junior high school bought several newspaper routes from neighborhood kids to create his first business. Mort is also the author of *Revenue Vs. Sales*, a three book series that you can find on Amazon.com.

Carly Greenberg attends the University of Maryland's Smith School of Business with a double major in marketing and management. Carly's twin brother has autism, and she has helped him find his voice through her unique interactions with him. He is the original little guy with greatness. Carly is the original fearless girl, always helping others, volunteering, and finding ways to do more with less - all while having to put up with a crazy dad. Carly also holds a black belt in Tae Kwon Do.

www.ingramcontent.com/pod-product-compliance
Lightning Source LLC
Chambersburg PA
CBHW052345210326
41597CB00037B/6260